By Some Miracle
A Year Lousy with Meteors

By Some Miracle
A Year Lousy with Meteors

Ariana-Sophia Kartsonis
Cynthia Arrieu-King

Dream Horse Press
Aptos, California

Dream Horse Press
Post Office Box 2080
Aptos, California 95001-2080

Copyright © 2013
All rights reserved

No part of this book may be reprinted without the express written permission of the publisher. For permissions, contact Dream Horse Press, Post Office Box 2080, Aptos, California, 95001-2080.
editor@dreamhorsepress.com

Printed in the United States of America
Published in 2013 by Dream Horse Press

ISBN 978-1-935716-23-5

Cover artwork:

Twos
by Rain Jordan
www.rainjordanart.com

Contents

Into the Celery Doors	7
By Some Miracle A Year Lousy with Meteors	8
The Gratitudes	9
Fox Shoots Hunter in Belarus	10
I am not happy with loss as an ethos	11
Dear Covered in My Tears	12
Windshelf	14
The Solitude of Smarts	15
Kathy Coles	16
The Gratitudes (II)	18
Quit Mooning Ezra	19
The Gold-Armoured Girl Reflects in a Closet	20
Man Tries to De-ice Porch, Sets House Afire	22
View From Claustrophobia	23
Photographed in Cold, Underdressed	24
Shoe-Tree	25
The Our of the Hour	26
Spilt Milk	28
Christmas	29
Planet Plaint	30
The Gratitudes (III)	31
Door to Where You're Going Next	32
Enormous Headline: Forget!	33

○   Into the Celery Doors

Around the bodega, its blunt black awning,
alstromeria, ronunculus trimmed to the ankle,
a quick break from the make-believe blue
blossoms to sandwiches on carts. A bus horn
and a busker's song braid inside refreshing chaos.
A white splotch hangs above emptiness. Iron-scent
touches the ticket-edge before a run down stairs:
the dream of monotony gone, heads ascending
to some nightish-above. Those maybes light pink signals,
a cardiology afloat over the wide whiteness,
cabs cabbed. Do you love the square
or sinking into bed more? It's hard to say which.
A cool green gate to pass under, a cool green pill
and bliss—your affection for waiting for two a.m. trains,
your goods wrapped in yesterday's *Times*. A bamboo grove
of guesses: Should I be on this side, or the other?
And your hair blows back in un-ironic gratitude for the violin screech,
a heart-shaped bit of light swimming to you through space.
The word city opens its silver-robe like a stick of gum and you let it.

◯   By Some Miracle A Year Lousy with Meteors

I have pressed my liver between panes of glass like
a souvenir shop wild aster. Several white gleams mark
the sun falling, no violet smoke to interrupt.

I have offered up meadows, the orbiting music some
galaxy covets, too far from me. And counting up blue
skies as if any number matched with this year.

I have whistled this year from a distance, a sound
only audible to hope, settled as milk. In the muscles
of other mammals, cold bowls its dirty,

the incomprehensible left kitchenly: a dry erase
board and a marker dried quiet. There is no
closure, there is no twine knotting shut bags

full of night, old biscuits, rage, gift wrap, Januaries,
pill bottles, a Whitman's nougat bitten in two.
Our un-recyclables piled and behind them, as though

behind a hill, a quiver shimmers. The bull faces
a man shooting arrows and the sun slid before
oily for target practice across innumerable birded

skies. The scrims move across, cardboard scenery
to represent air. Blue as grey, white as heat,
an atmosphere storms so slowly like an anteroom

and you listening for me to go up to bed,
my anteroom a chagrined charge, what we'll
always have, a shadow charges a string of pauses.

◐   The Gratitudes

For truffles, balloon animals, never-twice cloud-shapes, for towns we pass through called Vermillion, Canton, Medina, Xenia. For the Micelli Dairy, the Pumpkin Queen of Circleville, I develop an attitude. They develop orange auras, my hand stops itching altogether and a peaceful catastrophe calls me back to the audience. The words are too much with us—thank you, because we could not stop for debts—debts kindly stopped for me and the carriage of knowing what you have: a pie in the cupboard, enough.

◯   Fox Shoots Hunter in Belarus

Red weeds crinkling, a back taken up mountainous,
air burnt and sky wrinkled, a mountain backing up.

What is smoked but intention, feral quips, a fox
laying a delicate nose to the gun

a crack, the earth slides sideways,
gunpowder and fur collar, a momentary

level to the injured and injuring. A hunter
shot by his animal, what else can the sky laugh on?

Clap its blue to our surprise. What color
chosen for our ability to endure; to miss a shot,

to re-miss, to be remiss. One awkward feeling
altered with talk and love and instantly

another awful feeling springs up.
We forget ourselves—the beasts of us

and what feasts on our amnesia;
the color of sundown and mistake

the rusting slyness and true aim
untrue, then too, these good things of accident.

A wounded fox shot its would-be killer in Belarus by pulling the trigger on the hunter's gun as the pair scuffled after the man tried to finish the animal off with the butt of the rifle, media reported in January 2011. The unnamed hunter, who had approached the fox after wounding it from a distance, was in hospital with a leg wound, while the fox made its escape, media said, citing prosecutors from the Grodno region. "The animal fiercely resisted and in the struggle accidentally pulled the trigger with its paw," one prosecutor was quoted as saying.

◐   I am not happy with loss as an ethos

I am not happy with loss as an ethos.
Where did the leaves turn against me
except to fall away and what autumn this

if not yellow, orange, red meant to be
mere flame and not the ashing
on the shag rugs of my pitiful jubilation?

My habits barely furnished, a freedom
in nothing-doing and this holds
the mundane boxed up, it holes-in

and home is where the hard is. Difficult
temperatures, departures: the stayings
moreso. I've a habit of lingering too

long, a way with playing dread
and the movers outside the window.
We close the drapes on self-deceit,

and windows panel back across, allegro,
too many absent-minded combings
of hair touched with snow, her imitation

little hand held out for jokes, a feigned fear
of movie devils. Our bliss is purely cinematic
and what joy we inherit, we paint on the canvas

inherent before us. Call it sky, call it That Day
We Baked Lattice Cherry Pie, call it Largesse.
Say a happy day was not an accident.

◐   Dear Covered in My Tears

Those were the first hours of the year
back when I was optimistic and planned
hours out of synch: despair & boredom,
February. Those were the first books
filled with penciled birds nestled into
the bed, small creatures in nightcaps
squirreled away the hours both tree
webbed and spring-sky-gazing.

Saltines and plum jam: Those first ways
to count stripes red, nurture beside
the bed a small plant whose leaves
eased towards the sun that gave
heat—almost human. Light
sustained, as it was burning, as
it was blinding, as it lent sight.
There was no rain and I darkened
the times you pointed out the riven
clouds, purple and smeared as if
rain has no direction but us.

There was a first us, garden-
red, groomed. We sat utility fed,
saved our (choose one) coupons,
ticket stubs, selves, pennies. We saved, too,
our diner-straw-paper-sculptures,
dashed off notes to the market
lists like: apples, chowder, kisses, me.

Further off, a second set of us sat

under second dawns rosy with
afterthoughts. Footing gained
near a vibration of ruby trees,
then the third us meant we lost
footing. The trees ripened their
jeweled-innards and we watched
from some distant grove our next
selves throw picnics or balance
grapes over our mouths then
pull them laughing, away.

◯   Windshelf

A kite broad as a red square hung in a gold painting
and you listening.

The space between petals of the turbine,
he-loves-me-not and moving.

A soft thought opening my mouth to cold and its
improvements.

The underside of bluejays and jets.
Feeling buoyed up, in fall, the maple leaves a library

that dandelion spores pause against
before starrily descending

to where you are sitting. I lean to kiss your hair:
The air stands still for this.

○   The Solitude of Smarts

Ironies: Evolution scientists at Switzerland's University of Lausanne reported in June that over the course of 30 to 40 generations, ordinary flies tend to live longer if they're stupid. The researchers guessed that heightened neural activity overtaxed their systems.
                                          [Agence France-Presse, 6-4-08]

And isn't it the way, our way, getting into it
then having to fly out except, we're weary?
We're oil-slicked in our green-orange fire raincoats
and at the glass we bat ourselves, the panes
a fine thing to stun us. Lazy eights from dusk
to behind a shade and back: smallest calculators,
digits that refuse plain numerals. You wring
your hands and I can't say if you're cleaning
or simply praying a cellophaned wing or two
will lift you from your nightmare
where the meaning of life sends you
to-ing and fro-ing and the solitude of smarts
is a maggot-infested penny loafter, this life
of the mind, the young of our kind
and the yachts where the gods
keep their hideous pulivilli.

Kathy Coles

Canes and men walking straight into ponds like Magritte paintings.
Man with bowler, man with bowler, never tripping.
So I have to hang this awkward name around my neck
painted poppy red, and tired. *A* vehicle has room
for a breeze, a bird, and another. Why can't I
be *the* cheese? *The* cheese is at hand. *The* cheese is what
we're talking about, asleep on the checkered cloth. *A* cheese
travels by train and offends everyone with a smell that changes.

        And if one Kathy Cole walks into a bar with a poodle
        in her purse or a head full of so-Magritte sky
        what will the other Kathy Cole do who has just consumed
        her body weight plus eight poodles worth of rice
        and then lived to spite? How can one account for all the stray
        Kathy Coles waltzing by unclaimed, refusing to make eye-contact
        with what I've come to hope is the original, the Kathy Cole
        I dine with Wednesdays when a-drizzle with confusions-various.

Even that rice so anonymous, clinging to each other's grains
on this Wednesday bowl, not ceramic with fish but a woven
body running on bricks. Flesh, a washcloth
draped on to make the soul's
fever come down. That bastard definite article
elusive like some social number, the name
you have to have three passwords and birth-date for
so another Kathy Cole won't get your annuity, your down, your custom cake.

        But they will those clever Kathy Coles, I'll-tell-you.
        Why just last week—there goes one now!—one hopped
        the number 17 bound for we know not where and *the* Kathy Cole
        the Original, missed an appointment with her dentist
        or God or was it our lunch date—see Red Pepper
        and me there (no Kathy Coles but petulant) chopsticks poised
        like egrets & there goes she & she & she in cabs, on buses, one there
                on unicycle, a
        daffodil in one hand a passport in another and you guessed it—
        a forgery!—
                          oh sure it's *a* Kathy Cole

passport swinging as life goes down the road. I hear we've
got an art show opening, a literacy center program, a country
western song brewing about the lonesome. And leather

fringe, Coke bottle, and series, we have that private
dream of alone. Come down to the wire. Come down
to the mark, the fingerprint, the breath, the strange C in Cole
that bends back to cover the autograph from rain.

> Thread yourself where it matters, Kathies and Coles.
> In stadiums, in a city park, grocery store, where— swipe
> a card from your falling-apart wallet— the collective Cole
> savings goes down to the price of 12 eggs, 24 tea bags,
> 225 saltines in a box, and they drive home too, and start:
> dinner, one pot of tea, returning calls, weeping, kissing spouse
> off. One long draught of water from the tap for hot bath,
> the perfect sea for talking to God, requesting that one of us
> write the check, while another critiques the rain.

○   The Gratitudes (II)

Enough to have had so much to lose. Enough whipped cream on this morning's holiday latte to stock a strip club, enough with the tears, the stand-up comedians, the clown-phobias, the clowns. We've looked at clowns from both sides and with both kinds of mouths: smiles and the other way around. A simmering pan of sugar water; a simmering assortment of lights strung as seen through tears. Winding down, a smear of face paint and faux fur, a celebratory alarm clock announces the time: one noise that stops the thought you're disappointed. It's all here clattering when the train passes, every bone-china minute.

◐ Quit Mooning Ezra

Quit mooning, Ezra, what's botched is botched
and no cottaged-conscience undoes those songs.
The wrinkle in gone: who would fire a statue
of you in a bronze-eyed dusk? Thoughts
terza rima on the mind's sidewalk and wrongs
right nothing but their lean-tos. Sun slants
deceptively brighter, white glare leaving eyes
aching. And another cashed-out July sky

another summer eating itself up, one day
you'll want me for your taxidermy, but by then
the straw will have been cut off at the wrist.
What to fill the empty emptiness but
paper? A hollow body crammed with origami
cranes recalls flying dreams recalls empty
tents, a hot dirt-scented insomnia. A wilderness
of noises mistaken for lions, heat thieves,

and next noon, the dream rinsed; water—the least
expected passersby—grows something blossomed.
Grow something besides doubt, suspicion, grow something
from all this pulled-weed & stripped soil, grow something.

◐   The Gold-Armoured Girl Reflects in a Closet

Here, the darkness completes the rectangle, asks nothing of
the night but night-ness, asks nothing of nothingness   .
but derangement. A knowing begins as a coin behind
the eyes, not light exactly: inexactitude and
lightness? Here, the wherewithal appears in color.
A warp of hues, ribbon candy and spirit-mint

drops to a shoulder, pipes freezing overhead.
And braced against steel and in the face of colors, a girl
caught between idiot time and supper. Nauseated
with the endless seconds of childhood vistas, she pulls
the door to. It's a condition of wanting to re-create
northern light. There's the ting of hangers, a rabbit

softly away from the war and vacation rolled into one.
Hand on the knob, defeated by the largeness of others'
water glasses. A gold circle imagined as one clear curve
disappearing while another acute listen glints
eleven rings in this mental light. Worms pulled from the ground
and the classmate explaining the stress of leaving

the earth made their worm hearts swell so she took
a nail to them. In this average closet, was a recalled life
all one thing? Or was it sweat breaking out on water-glasses
minus the past? She pushes the door open enough to study
the photograph, leaning her forehead on the doorjamb.
The women so at its border, the middle too gray,

too vacant to describe. Yet she can take being shut
in homes sometimes. Cold is mostly devout,

the sweaters still snug in plywood chest. She'd seen
but never spoken to the meat at supermarkets, only
her mother saying yes or no to small pale animals
made of cookie. In an oval of sun, she picks the red beads

strung on trimmed wire slowly so they don't clatter,
and studies the clustered diamonds she shouldn't hold.
Square-root shoes, matched and mated, deferring
to navy tights inside nets, she finds precise wet ice
passed down and hidden in the green cloth box, and from
its sides senses the actual outsides of houses and herself.

○   Man Tries to De-ice Porch, Sets House Afire

The yard threatens the hedges.
A bit of purple dawn in the ice,

black and thick. The blowtorch
offered like a lighter in admiration

at a rock concert, the bright idea a singer:
melt all dangers. How isn't it that

every immolation begins frozen,
a thought coiled, a reach

for lighter or match
and winter ignites—

eaves first—vinyl pressed
to its highly flammable insulation.

Fraught intention, hollow fire:
all around him ice in a mockery

ice hissing ignorance, ice suggesting
what's meant to burn, holds.

He leans the blue and white flame
toward a guess: ice for injury,

ice for unrest. And lifting the torch
he notices heat against his back.

◯   View From Claustrophobia

Blue plastic capsule centered, swung.
The ferris wheel still, surrendered. Tourists
risen, or swaying down stopped
so long that they've taken to recall,
then to count the concentric
stone-thrown ripples in the pond
of the tree's heart. Their ride drew
ages on air before the wheel stopped.
How many oak years were they
before the tree of their day stopped growing?
Mentioning fingernails snagged on prayers,
the horizon sinking and rising,
a blue and gold brocade laid out
street-level. A culture formed:
and in that last hour, vertiginous
life, swinging or hanging still
might be their always. They
begin to forget dinner plans, jobs
and the mailbox that gathers the story
of discounts. Now they all Ferris wheel
a continent, its islands shining eyes—
the frightening thing knowing one
could be seen by raptors, God, unknowing
freedom, and an electric current
that might be the brain's frantic firing,
the dead-sputter of the wheel.
Or them: their spider-vision looking back.

◐   Photographed in Cold, Underdressed

The bon mots crushing my spine, I'm fine,
though missing street-kissing in black and white

the Paris of the mind, this string of people
mouthing mints. Twenty minutes to catch

an international flight, I get a tricycle
and sweep up hair along the way.

The glamorous distance, accelerated,
exhilarated begins to think my arms white

willow branches. In full summer, a house's
trim painted to crusts, maize in the draped

window, and I'm craving certain scorn,
lateness a pane so good it almost

makes me cry. The harder I pedal
with luggage on my back, the faster I run

down a concourse, the further my French
outruns me. Glass doors shift. Planes roar gray.

◯   Shoe-Tree

Of the feet in the air, millions aloft
and what heaven can be crossed
and survived, is crossed with each wind;
Walk the loneliest road to get to the center
of an idea; walk the loneliest square of air
the first pair catches in branches.

Dual trophies hung like two caught ears strung up
listening. A desert blows in like flexed wheat,
sod silent. Then the next lone traveler
thinks skyly, thinks message on the sole,
considers the way a thing we wear wears
us back. Pomade in the crown.

Thunder in our step. Too few leaps.

Somewhere in a movie, an airport shoeshine
and the dialogue: Two kinds of people: those who try
to climb the sky, and those who cut them down.

In the difference a half-morning makes, a mourning
and what was laced to the ether unties
itself from the boundless blue
and turns to binding blues
unlike a musicbox ballerina,
unlike a beloved, rundown sneaker
one runner on a mobile spins left, then right
with the passing breeze

◯   The Our of the Hour

Dear Happening Awaiting an Accident. Dear Grove of Balloon Trees Blooming.
When I said the word *our*, meaning belonging to us, you confused the term as
a canopy once again hovering over me and the someone who skipped my heart
across a summer's lake
I probably hadn't used the first person plural possessive even once those past
months to mean me and anyone else's anything.

December your call. You'd just been to the zoo which they'd strung in Christmas
lights and opened for the night. The ducks turned into black paper cut-out ducks
silhouetted on the pond. The cat-tails looked art-deco. I remember.

Dear Stowaway in any Similar Shipwreck. Dear Christmas
Ornaments for Drag Queens.
Dear Any-Luster-Seeker, the thing is, certain nights humid, netted with mosquito
hum and vampiric intentions, I know why.

Every day was a festival.
The trees were hung with fruits made of little white lights
and I walked over the bridge and the one-armed bandits
everywhere were ringing with minor wins.

Dear Money. Dear Cherry-Bell-Bar. Dear Gamblers Everywhere,
take the casino by storm with your bright nickels, your fat wallets,
your lean hearts. All fall I've tried to tell you about how we were

the our of every hour dusking across the clockface of every casino
everywhere.
Under that forever-evening sky and timeless ourselves,
it's always early enough to chance a win, to cut our losses,
to wager every hour
on an our that might prove rich enough for spending the better part
of always alongside. So Friend, call me a pitbull angel or call me
when you need reminding about these hours that parade themselves
in cities where lovers run away from the time for a time and I'll tell you a story

about a grove of trees I wandered into one perfect August always-night,

and what was ripening then, turned to dazzle and what was dazzle turned away,
but not before we gorged ourselves on peaches and plums and apples

made of nothing but serious volumes of the luminous and not before
we shone and shone and shone enough to almost make abandoning
that perfect artificial night for a heavy, fruitless dose of the other sky
worth the coins we fed until we played ourselves out.

○   Spilt Milk

What greasy-finding, what avalanche of dairy-white fiction
misread, how the mind goes Milosz at the phrase milk-spill,
the earth's hills rolling in skeins of white
   a calcium blanket, the ugly gulls
       in their milk-coats.

What divides this land is white foam
an absurd line of miniscule bubbles
the warm milk frothing at the mouth
hint of wind, hint of grass. They never cry
over this much of it, and skimming the horizon
whole, a morning's full-fat relief map, creamy.

Then we slept free with no help;
we saw at the end of a road
men trying to sweep a lake of milk,
the uses of empty sky and tears.

Griffith claimed that new EPA rules treat milk spills the same way they treat oil spills. He titled the newsletter "Crying over spilt milk."

"What do spilt milk and oil have in common?" he wrote. "Quite a bit, according to the EPA. In fact, a new ruling by the EPA would force dairy farmers to comply with the Spill Prevention, Control and Countermeasure Program when dealing with spilt milk -- the same regulations oil and natural gas producers must follow. The EPA's reasoning is that milk contains 'a percentage of animal fats, which is a non-petroleum oil.' It appears spilt milk is just as threatening as an oil spill."

With visions of dairy farmers delicately dabbing milk off the wings of ducks, we looked into the claim.

Beth Breeding, Griffith's press secretary, said her boss's information came from the EPA's website. So we went there.

Right away, we found problems with Griffith's claim. The website says milk has been regulated under the Spill Prevention Control and Countermeasure program since 1973, when the Clean Water Act took effect. The law was passed by Congress the preceding year over the veto of Republican President Richard Nixon. So this is hardly a "new ruling," as Griffith says. It has been in effect for 38 years.

◐ Christmas

It is time to write the poem. To make the donuts.

To scrawl a foil intention into the scenery.

To send a jaunty cobalt dress that looks very you.

The boiling revelation before forking flour into a bowl.

A red shimmer jolts between the fir's arms.

We gave up toiling in darkness, trying to articulate vast gardenias of eventuality.

Pausing to nap and dry my terribly eh spiritual socks,

I know it's easier than ever to measure sandy joy

in spoons of warmed-up jam. A heated thought

rinses through the mind, hot tea. The reflective

maps-of-consciousness fold shut as we clink our mugs.

◐   Planet Plaint

Even in an empty room, a sound
                like the inner sea of a shell.
In the cellar the onions contain weeping,
                even the eyes of the potatoes well-up,
an orange rise in the wall.
                Widths of tiny bells ringing, that music
Dust hums a low bass. Dark matters,
                mostly as a place to think.
Four days without speaking
                to anyone, the sun bleaches in
from seas to shining seize
                the constellation of confessions
wrinkles; a twin.
                And then hearing the sphere's music
from some other's point
                of view leaves you a sigh

◐   The Gratitudes (III)

China-minute, porcelain hour; nevertheless, a clock takes it in the face every time. Expectation mothers a nude. A hip nipped, and gratitude. Give thanks for the breakable-recollection, practice the two-step, electric slide, the jitterbug, merenge and the take-it-in-stride. The turn-the-other cheek-tango, a hand on your hand pulling you through the turn, sweeps up, sweeps down, another hour gone. And a minute minute set deep in a green dip, a swoop where the swoon meant to be. You bend your knees, your twin-beliefs, and every step feels like prayer.

○   Door to Where You're Going Next

That can't be a portal, so what knob waits unturned?

What yellow light turns red and then green
and we are all out of primary colors?

In this town, turn the page, the corner, the key
and what was yours becomes a box of old shoes.

Magazines, that spice rack that looks
like a dozen eyes into the grey, or

Carmen Mirandas rendered in salt dough,
a velvet Elvis sucked dry of its irony.

A truncated thought, what pile should this
go to? Trash? Charity? The friend who likes

adopted homes and runners, the change
your friend envies as a new page. But you

recall the way this last city reluctantly
handed out language you never loved. Still—

you know the day the market marks cherries down,
asparagus, the best bakery for baguettes, another for rye.

◯   Enormous Headline: Forget!

The simple ferns grave and curled, holding dew, mirror
the nestling's ribcage, the shape of hands moving away
after holding other hands. The wisteria's defeat,
the plane tickets to Venezuela un-torn. What wind,
what heat rising into a cloud and shifting all to hell?
Stop asking questions. Stop switching from future

to past tense so swiftly you send the unopened mail
flying. A bee stinger easily plucked out. And then
you wait the way summer bent itself over your childhood,
a nap taking you out. The noisy air pre-thunderstorm

sounds a warning. You hear foghorns and drift off to sea.
You sit on a wave, sitting in eternity. A sun waves
pink scarves and the horizon dozes against breathiness

and a yellow sweet perfume. As sweet as bleeding gold
can be, and the present wipes you with the clean rag breeze

      erasing as much as it reveals

Acknowledgments

"Windshelf": *Black Warrior Review*
"This Year Lousy With Meteors": *Boston Review*
"Kathy Coles": *Court Green*
"Obey Gravity": *New Orleans Review*
"The Our of the Hour." *Poetlore*

The authors would like to thank Red Pepper and the University of Cincinnati in Cincinnati, Ohio.

www.ingramcontent.com/pod-product-compliance
Lightning Source LLC
Chambersburg PA
CBHW032008060426
42449CB00032B/1218